Writing 25

The publication of this book was supported by a grant from the National Endowment for the Arts in Washington, D.C., a federal agency created by an Act of Congress in 1965.

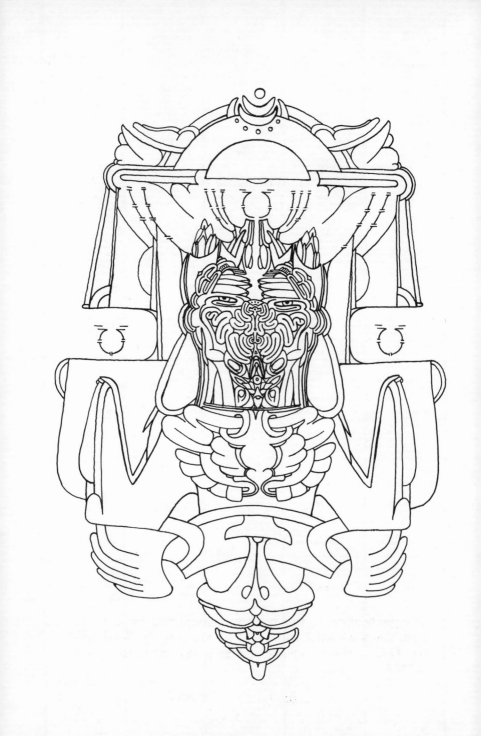

Philip Lamantia

THE BLOOD OF THE AIR

Four Seasons Foundation

San Francisco   1970

9/1972
Genl.

Several of these poems were first published in *Penguin Modern Poets* 13, *Anti-Narcissus*, and *Point-Vergule*

Library of Congress Catalog Card Number: 74–105925
Standard Book No.: 0–87704–013–3

Cover photograph by Stanley Reade

Also by Philip Lamantia:
  Selected Poems, 1943–1966
  Touch of the Marvelous

The Writing Series is edited by Donald Allen and published by Four Seasons Foundation, 1815 Jones Street, San Francisco, California 94109

Distributed by Book People, 2010 Seventh Street Berkeley, California 94710

for Nancy
at the secrets
of the marvelous

TO THE READER
I am not the I who writes,
but the eye is ours that parts the fire
in things unseen and then, seen.

"LAMANTINES:

A species of herbivorous mermaid-like mammals native to Africa and the Americas, inhabiting the mouths of larger rivers. They play, in West-African myth, a role similar to that of the Sirens in Europe."

—Lilyan Kesteloot: *Les Écrivains Noirs de Langue Français*

Contents

Frontispiece drawing by Marie Wilson

THE LIBRAN AGE

I Touch You   3
"You wait you wail"   6
Altesia or the Lava Flow of Mount Rainier   7
Blue Locus   8
The Talisman   10

FLAMING TEETH

"Open your head of cisterns"   13
"San Francisco melts as I come together"   14
"The maginot line of poetry has not been invented"   15
"With the opening of light in my soul"   16
Ephemeris   17
Out of My Hat of Shoals   18
Smile Berries   20
Fantast   21
The Faery Chambers   22
Seattle   23
"Little hole of black hallucination on the wall"   24
"The mosque of your eye has exploded"   25
Horse Angel   27
The Comics   28
Tonight Burned with Solar Slime   30
Flaming Teeth   32

Penetrant Tumors   38
The Analog   41
World without End   42

Four automatic drawings by the poet   5, 19, 29, 40

". . . The whole thing, for Surrealism, had been to convince ourselves we had put our hands on the "primal matter" [*matière première*] (in the alchemical sense) of language; after that, to know *where* to find it and, needless to say, without interest in reproducing it to the point of satiety; this is said for the benefit of those who are surprised that among us the *practice* of automatic writing was so quickly abandoned. Up to now it has been asserted that the confrontation with the products of this writing aimed the projector on the region where desire arises unconstrained, which is also where myths take wing. One can not insist enough on the meaning and scope of the operation which tended to restore to language its true life: rather than go back again from the thing signified to the sign surviving it (which, in any case, would prove to be impossible) it is best in one leap to look back to the birth of that which signifies. The spirit which renders such an operation possible and even thinkable is none other than that which has always animated occult philosophy and, according to which, from the fact that expression is at the origin of everything it follows that 'the name must *germinate,* so to speak, or otherwise it is false.' The principal contribution of Surrealism in poetry as in the plastic arts is to have so sufficiently exalted this germination that everything other than it seems ridiculous."

—André Breton: *Of Surrealism in Its Living Works* (1953)

The Libran Age

I Touch You

I touch you with my eyes when you lie under spiders of silk
I touch you with my one hundred headed giraffes too secret to
   be seen
the rods & cones the morning covets awaken you
with my touch of tobacco eyes
and you rise from the snail's bed of tubular hair
I touch you with the breath of jet planes
and they are gone elsewhere to touch you too
I won't have you touched by sordid saints
I touch you with the hour that drips scent
snared from the chain of immaculate lice
who avenge themselves forever on the holy of holies
I touch you with the wind heaving the breasts of the morning
I touch you in the overcrowds
and they vanish
replaced by all the women who resemble you
and I touch them with the eyes of the sun

Annihilation of priests
I touch you on the threshold of the totem
carbon salt on the breath of the world
I touch you with my intricate rose superior to the fog
I touch you with heart strings of the veiled mountain
whose magnetic moment is the sight of us making love

I rend your skirt by the wind stolen from ancient castles
your legs secrete the essence of wheat
and your ankles brush the wing of crow
Your lips touch alchemic gold torn from the femur bone of
     poetry
whispering through archives of your smile
that beguiles the oracle who has a headache to change his
     legends
I touch your earlobe with the fatal elegance of the peacock lip
your convulsions gallop my heart of the rose hermetic and
     flushed by goats sighting prey
I touch your nipples
that touch heaven that is all of you touching me
the temple of your hips
the morning glory of your sex
the miracle of bedsheets and the sacrament of sweat

Rhythms of your thighs are the music of the spheres

You are more beautiful than the black buttocks of dawn
and all light has been given to veil you from the murderers of
     love

I touch your presence undressing the furniture
whose cries fill the distance between us
and you shall hear
when I touch you with telepathic tendrils
for then I'll come into you the light of the waking dream

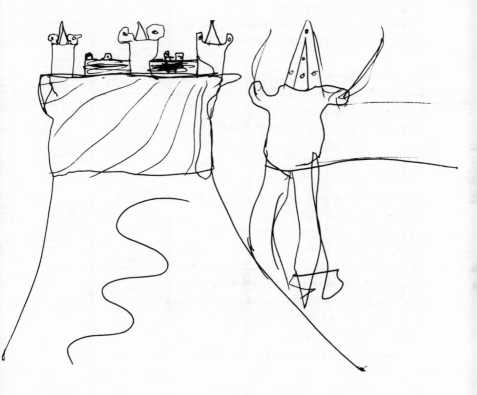

You wait you wail
Across the silences
That are a struggle in the world
Obstacles said to be conjunctions of Saturn and the Moon
Objects—telephones—are taboo
Taboo the sky curled into leaden pillars
Taboo the river of racing horses

The sun spits on my fingers
Your little finger completes a sentence
Solitude is a flame of sleep
Jungles fold me in passionate bird omens

Where are you

The page is turning against me like a wave of horses
I'm unsteady on this continent
That throws its chains around all of us
As if we weren't here
Orbiting like apples through galaxies of desire
Your countenance in the clock I map
And your hands brushing the hair invisible
Step by step we come closer
To the Thunderbird's retreat
And beauty cries from a lacerated heart

Altesia or the Lava Flow of Mount Rainier

You are come to me like fondling depths I'm at the Pont-Neuf
Say I shackle and unshackle the meat drippings of art
A threshold of owl eyes spanning Mount Olympus
Turning coat tails and hood menageries of certain Parisian
    streets
The grave look sizzling pages of Nicholas Flamel's lost book

I would free the prison snarling from your feet

Your smile is my hurricane
And the ache of traversing San Francisco with guillotines of
    history
At every intersection North Beach to Mission Dolores

A gilt-edged XIXth-century edition of Edward Young's *Night
    Thoughts* opens in your hair
        What if it were
My turn at blindman's bluff and you were "it"
Running over a gigantic mirror
        On a cow field in Normandy

Blue Locus

It's here the glove attacks the hand
Everything is splendidly distant
your torso carved out of daylight
on the screaming horizon I've ceased to hear
because you secrete a whisper and the clouds tremble

The squirrel you feed is the familiar of halos
trailing your thoughts from the spirit lake
blue locus
promising the unknown on a hike to the woods

There must be a playroom of totems
under the lake you raise with the key by which you read my lips
On the fur road you travel
I'm to steal the squirrel's eye
. . .which is how the sun looks when asleep . . .
and nail it over the photoglyph
in the space where you've cropped your head off

I want to play fanatically over your daylight
see the thunder-bridge return to the font
and bring you to where the dream emanates
through the paper-shackling reality
full optics
drenched with the juice of chance

O my lady of combustible cameo
your mouth of the northern lights
doubt's ease
and our blistering profanations
no more answers
you are writing the poem

who burn me with your shadow
that your body veils wet arrows
the birds that circle you
       breastplates
  for the army of love

The Talisman

Only for those who love is dawn visible throughout the day
and kicks over the halo at the pit of ocean
the diamond whirls
all that's fixed is volatile
and the crushed remnants of sparrows travel without moving

I find myself smoking the dust of myself
hurled to the twilight
where we were born from the womb of invisible children
so that even the liver of cities
can be turned into my amulet of laughing bile

Melted by shadows of love
I constellate love with teeth of fire
until any arrangement the world presents
to the eyes at the tip of my tongue
becomes the perfect food of constant hunger

Today the moon was visible at dawn
to reflect o woman the other half of me you are
conic your breasts gems of the air
triangle your thighs delicate leopards in the wood where
    you wait

Flaming Teeth

Open your head of cisterns
Let fly the soft iron imbibing your mummy
This is the golden age
Walking overnight across the united states a state of mind like
   any other
Open your head of windmills
Let fly the queen of spades and the masked man of the sabbat
Be friendly to Cotton Mather take ether fly past the moon
Open your head of sallow dreams
Let fly the first mare the one come from the Azores
The second mare shall wear her breakfast as a turban
The third one the third one shall conquer Asia with icecream
Make up your mind whether to turn black or red
I kick over a high-rise apartment in my room
And what do you do steel eagle
Is the waterfall in your eyes burning
But a moment now and the hands of empire shall wither
Having dug the graves of the future the poor shall be walking in
   mailsuits
I have a window eating fog there's a riot on Alcatraz Island
The streets of chinatown are still adventurous I met an opera
   singer in my raw fish salad
She was on her way to sing Puccini to the Vietnamese
Open your head and find Narcissus there and strangle him it's
   perfectly legitimate
Let fly the churches of memory they're only prisons anyway

San Francisco melts as I come together
There's no need for music
I calm the waves of galactic eyes
We are everywhere at once
Like the fond palm leaves of my childhood
That broke from my breast of stars
O night of incandescent water bugs
Tulips dahlias and lupines hunt the bread of rain
"The Three Graces" in my father's garden magnets of my brain
Their faces light up the pool of nirvanic stratagems
Dissolve into the blood of the air

Fireflies and tiger lilies crash on white horses
Through the cruel landscapes Mrs Radcliffe's Pyrenees have
    their throats of bandit geography
Slit open by the fetid atmospheres of demonic chemistry
The vengeance of the Adepts may be at hand for those who
    blew up petunias
Palingenesis be my watermark
Whatever you mean Overthrow the world
The slap of Urania across reality's face
These gems of violent youth trickle down the nude breast of the
    woman I love
Are the thunder pins of water
Stephen Schwartz says I resemble an iguana
We chance encounter ourselves in slanting parks of San Fran-
    cisco
The Ibis bird our talisman
As waves of little fiery lips lap up our ancestors
Under the eye of Horus Tremendous Convulsions
       We shall go out
           Transparent as the Devil

The maginot line of poetry has not been invented
Working on railroads of Hymettus honey the traps are set
This wavering pinnacle to transparent fire bleeds on alembic
water
Giantess o giantess
Your husk of sleep
Stretches my burning skin
No one is free
This area of freedom opens the basilisk's belly full of rotting
books
Priests of literature float under the Ganges
Mahatmas descend from their hotbeds with the rattling skull
With zabaglione soaked in meatball sauce
Chinese mustard leaks from their temples that's all
Are we going through the door where the dead smile smiles of
dolls
Manikins come alive
Their livers suckable as plums and raging stars
A garment flows on Grant Avenue
Forever to trap the visiting collars
That broke teeth on holy breads
Lucky money changes a monocle for a rose of salt
Genius pins us with the tieclip of despair
Joy beckons revolutionary ladies for the grand éclair
Two steps back or forward it makes no difference

With the opening of light in my soul
What more and how I swim free except the whole cemetery rise
    with me
There are no heights in the sparkling islands
My flesh rolls into the first refuge
Across the dawn's belly
Also opening along with the cranking metals of the city
Its soul of splintered being
   Its knobs of celestial systems
      And its look of wizard pigs

Hope rules out the equipoise of kings
I run into my friends coming out of drugstores which always
    know the time according to comic gorgons
That slip as powders into the air of imaginary bombs

The toilets are sleeping
And the fist of charms runs down streets deserted by its martyrs
Where one day
The cruel Whip shall find its anvil to wed the Dawn

Ephemeris

The room has lips to speak antediluvian wishes
      cloud wing of forest
        carbonic eye from the sea
The child has lost his way and found
His human breakfast table fast by the coral'shore
Morning scales the mountain
With the palpitating flower I found in my mailbox
      unknown hydra service
        aerolith express

The conjurations at noon on the streets of the most industrious
    cities
For the advent of purple arachnids
For a rain of butterflies
The simultaneous apparition of flame-lined ladies from the
    cedar beds of the future

    X Magician
      at once to seed the air
        with musk giants
Clouds grow so softly under your skirts
I can watch the children climbing the diamond temples at every
    corner
And there's a taste of bituminous wine
For the solar incubation so rarely conjured
But for your hair shedding the stars
    O little girls of the forest of cities

Out of My Hat of Shoals

Out of my hat of shoals
Mixed ladies in a park of seals
Transvestite fire and wink of water
Green flame rapes the garden tulips
Trees of nonsense bend their songs
Lips of clouds and kites of pain
I'm at a shower of windows
All the houses are made of rain
No more speed   we float
I'm happy with hermetic games
The toys of sleeping mathematicians
Triangles and compass of water
Theorems beyond reason
Hypnotic ladies read the future with the sweat of roses
I comb the stars
And they undress the moon with their nipples
The hunt is on
No one will ever sleep again
Sweet music of epicene bodies
All is pregnant with mystery
And the idols have been eaten up
Marigolds fume in the night
The day is locked in a box at sea
The sun has finally married the moon

19

Smile Berries

My lines of light fungusstone of hatemill and showers of love
Beyond these categories
Finally no name
Avalanche of scent
Pungent cinnamon spray
Pumice foam flower

Fear not children to skate
Through your happy dart of a wish
Even if it kills your parents
Better to hurt the dead than salt the young

We're off into ourselves
Every moment is light
I eat the sun I scale the moon

There are diamonds through the lattice of perfumes I steal from
    your hair
Wild apples war on the pickers
Their hands scorched by flames of white juice

The cherries will never fall except through baskets
And all the markets empty with human products

The better to drink them with I say
                          Smile berries for sale

Fantast

From a jet plane window I landed into an eighteenth-century
  drawing room
Where the Marquis de Sade and I were of one mind tasting
  pineapples
Cameo brooches burst and showered us with pomegranate
  fumes
From the wrists of Doctor Mesmer little commercial empires
  sprouted sent on slow boats to Boston Harbour
Where I'm smoking Copley Square by the laughing wheels of
  the trains of totemic beasts
Spirit-lined
I proclaim the empire of molten man one with all his precious
  stones
The trees of America light up the specters of Cotton Mather
Happily we shall live my hair burning the snow
My eyes burning forever over the Rockies Hello Chief Seattle

The Faery Chambers

The stereophonic angelic beauty à la Landini
O to be back in the frost-bitten middle ages
And away under the smoldering carbons
Spitting with Grunewald's demon
In the rose-soaked nights of the patient alchemist
Guido Guerci another sicilian subtly flooding the north with the
    theoria of colors at Isenheim
My eyes at the vision of diatonic numbers Blue the wind
Crimson the flight
Green the whorl of recalcitrant ladies
The dip harmonies
Harp honey
Oh for the slow tambourines I hear in the belfries of Adepts
The high seriousness of Basil Valentine's *Triumphal Chariot of
    Antimony*
Never again in chemistry until Fulcanelli
All writ by The Master "A"
                    across the façades of cathedrals
On the parvis am I again
The daily news cracked open from ecstatic faces at Santiago de
    Compostela
This is very dark my pitiful rams
And there are heavy ferous boots ferous horses ferous wars were
    preached
Everything went down the draining nose of Pope Innocent the
    Third
And Alexander the Bull gave the coup de grâce where gnomons
                    lurked in Fra Pacioli's double-column book-
                    keeping machine
The Emperor Frederick Secōndo revived the ancient questions
    out on that parvis
Turning on the stereo record
                            beat of my heart to their harps

Seattle

I'm passing through this city with a smile of smoke
There's no one around but giant plastic tubes
Eat the mountain and slay the dragons
It's all the same slipping over venomous skirts on fire
The tubes whisper El Dorado with neon haematoids for teeth
Little homunculi and spaghetti dining cars
Dissolving dollars
I'm passing out in this city where the streets are jangling
    metaphysics the epidemic future propelled from Antares
I'm ordering sauerkraut with legs
Because I'm absent minded about the celestial weather
Very chilly between the ladies' chinchilla and her eyebrows are
    full of dragon books
The leaves of which I won't say spill but leak petunias
Better to take an apartment in the mountain at a high rent from
    the absent landlord
Stop Gorgeous Volatile
No one'll get out of here if I can help it without committing
    guilt without relish
The rites of guilt I say
The rites of guilt come with cans of soup and crisp gardens
Slain under the snowdrift pain Vetch the gorilla his name

Little hole of black hallucination on the wall
Tell me your secret bone of wisdom
Stuck as I know you are
                    Little black hole in the wall
Within the salt essence of reality
And if you don't
The craters of all the women I've loved shall throw their veiled
    lights on you
And into oblivion you go

                    Sibyl
Who opened her breast of infinity
The great gaping thunder flared its edible diamond
The sirens of her eyes surpass those of our ears
The place of love and the place of transmutation have met in the
    igneous air
Buildings have toppled into cups of grenadine or wine clouds
I have brushed feather sparks of blonde hair and discovered
    America

The mosque of your eye has exploded
Cathedrals with holes where shine the popes in their abortion of
    winged doubles
Your feet spread like vibrant chords over rustling plastic dolls
Bleeding american flags planted into your eyes knit with nazi
    stars
Leather brassieres wave through the universal televisions
Erupting Mount Rainier Popocatepetl and your eyes
Until the world's secret magicians yell
        "Please mend the buttons of my eyes"

Fall down with yogic tantrums my viper
Stare into Fifth Avenue through the flesh of Vietnam tingling
    with communist hair smuggled on airplanes from Java
Go back into the future
Watch the wind suck up the Kremlin
Get to work under the crotch of His Holiness Baboon Baby
Get high at the suntan hideaway of the Presidential Arm
Trigger your blood with toothpaste and vanishing paint
Commune daily with the columns of Graeco-Roman America

Into your slit-level underwear of the paranoiac cowboy
Dance lightfooted into your eyes
Look back into windows circling your heart of Indian beads
This is the end of silence you say
Sitting on all sides of the Atlantic facing the Pacific

Behemoth on the waters goes by
Advertising the lost books of Messiah Jesus von Heigelhauffer
Who is very interested in LSD rosebuds
NO EXPLANATION printed on suction cups of the mountains
    of the earth
Announces
        "Heaven is last night's orgasm
        Save yourself by finking on the Earth to the Moon"

AND
"Be sure to get yourself plenty of pocketsize torture machines
    made by humanoid toads
Who've computered themselves into a multiple population
    bible
Awash
With the bottle tops of your eyes"

Horse Angel

This word or this image
Whether the immense void to be filled from the ancients to now
Or the nightmare mane staring with crazy hypnotic starving
    eyes
Out of the oftseen painting of Blake's friend Fuseli
Don't know
But am tied to a thousand grecian pillars their horse nostrils
    migrating
And the stillness does not inflict any ice on their great hairs

      An upside-down Golden Fleece

The horse pervades
Horses superior to machines
Horses lighted with blue oil flame from the factories
It falls on them
Like an atom bomb on any andalusian field
It explodes not
Just the blue oil flame that's its metaphor

Horses watch me from my travels and metamorphose into mules
Transmigrating continents
      The donkey at Tangier
      And his burro on the road to Tamazunchale
      The road mendicant who was a giant of solar light Blind
        Indian
      And the moorish woman with the campesino straw hat
        sitting on a bag of esparto grass
All horse cultures
And the horse in dreams!
If I could speak of their manes hanging like metals
Hoofs tapping the rocks
And that wild look straight ahead in a fertile valley
                    the sun

The Comics

Cussing
the men are going home to work
on sleeping horses
and automobiles come alive
and return to the factories
wearing lingerie and makeup
Steering wheels chrome fenders and gears
leer at the computers
in the outer offices
and the engines—ah those seductive engines—
get into black boots and thrash the clouds
rushing through gargantuan windows the pistons are eating
with anthropoid teeth

The scimitar of the
antediluvian wastes

Baroque tungsten

Genuflecting chrome rivers

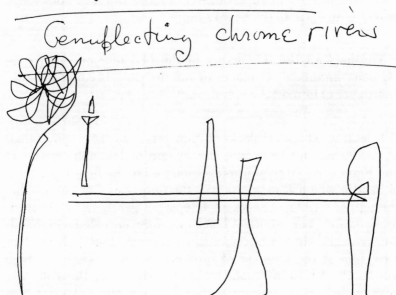

Tonight Burned with Solar Slime

Tonight burned with solar slime tonight flung from the space station tonight purveyed by lugar vendors tonight the umbilical cord of this torrent of words.

You are no more the sinister angel but the white killer dressed in carnation milk. Your 12-year-old lips refuse the black dinner and the nun you raped is severely punished by the mallet of madness. I swim free. Nevertheless. Exiles. The tough nut of the night bolts the window on my dream more personal than what you think you may become or ever were. Pea brain is the star's octopus sucker or is not to be disturbed; to sleep, a poet Awakened on the shed of super-malachites and the luminous lodge *gained* is an entry to the beard's fame.

The hook of the telephones of the bed tear out your song "Cruelty annulled" O pincer of the invisible become the concrete layer of immortal conundrums.

I dedicate the rant blocks of New Jersey to the phony canals of California and viceversa; the solemn melancholic towers of San Francisco join their armless tomatoes to the floating cisterns of Seattle which I imagine carve the totems of Columbus Ohio through a visible network of telepathic geometry *That landscape on fire.* The mouth of black men forever sealed with heraldic signs and the snobbery of lost kingdoms found themselves New Life at the moment of supreme sacrilege when the blue iron teeth of false messiahs return to reign over the Potomac, long exploding its impure timber through the universal face owned by 100,000 poets I am or can be if only you, serpent from the inner mines, unload your main highway through the same state with no stop signs tattooed on the absence of public statuary. Though the state is perfect if gone to by the road that can not end ever into you, eternal sleeper, who awaken in the automatic trance: this trajectory to everywhere I oracle, mania outfield pitched to the cyclone's rebirth.

Flaming Teeth

The earthquake slivers
The broken nails of the nazis
Mister Fly and his obsidian mask
My father on his razor
Basalt nightmares
Megalithic godplanes click the xylophones
My wracking spit spits
Words are magic beans
Children of the flat-faced musicians
Cross the street into subtropical ice
Manuring down your hand split a hundred ways
By the onyx of baptism
Stop
I'm climbing
To genocide the look of you
A thousand shacks
Human faces
Synthetic clouds
O for the slaughter America pinned on its bottom
I'd give up the rasp of Europe
Beatific visions sprawled on coat hangers
And weigh the silence with real screws
The fists of dawn
I'm still too intelligent
Become waste of years
Cruel whistling from under the snow inside the floorboards
And asleep drugged poet
You're safe striking the buttocks of the dream machine

Endless
Filth
Phanes

With the 24 electromagnetic

With rich tongue doorway briar and the lost look of Astatara
With bleeding pens
Dracula coins are the final exchange
"M" on all the rooftops signs the invisible with your blood
    imperial
And no more tempests in the tombs
Put them to sleep with the war angels
Which are all the angels

●

I'm a monster in my work plates
Over glades of dark statues that churn your retina priests of the
    Drag
And the dust I clean my sugar with
Knock down smoke over the everglades I'm american as rusting
    rain poltergeist salami
And a hundred tongues at once
Bumble Bee Heaven's my name
Cycling in graves
Little Joy Rider stuck her prehensile gibberish
Into the orbitic Tilt Mechanism freely bestowed by the papal
    party
That secretly seduced the swollen ash
From which six billion shadows stood up
Every dictator I've invented
And dried up the oceans

Drifting in my green dope cellar dream
Mother of black immaculates and sneezing scapulars
With the senatorial poets elect
With sting ray for breakfast
Juggling the clouds and weeping O the mystery of so many
    centuries

Art with its capitols
Imitating animal sounds
Went by
For this disquietudinous feather languishing infinity on a pedes-
     tal of shoes
All the images of Jesus were slapped together like Israel
And all was cool in the opium fields
Panama was still born from eagles of Hydra
There were so many birds bursting the hinges of Our Lady
She was hallucinated on the clever spot the Son chose
The Electric Decretal Caesar-christus

In and out of the valley of death
The valley of death
Little invisible bibles saying "How do you do, are the rare cli-
     mates moldy today?"
Just then the surgeon general master initiate
Slunk from his vatlined shroud of history
Imhotep—Voltaire—his name—
Would you believe it?
I'm going to go to sleep

•

I shall say these things that curl beyond reach
A fatal balloon
Resolving riddles
It's pure abyss-crackling vortex

And silence opens her lips very much like arson

•

Tomb rise
And it sees a vision of beauteous sexual bags
And the caravan of flutes drops its melons over the sands I am
    not
Into the fog I am
The infinite I become
With mad hands scraping the jewel of my hideaway
To rise to the black pinnacle Roman empires of thought
Fly down fast and around Amitabha
A succession of literary images cabalas insecticides
Nail your heart here

Stone windows grate their teeth
And the processions are inside secret rooms
The death ravens chatter

I won't let the precision instruments bite me
I'm obsessed by death fantasies

There's this silken road
Down here I can invent the moth to kill memory
Flay it alive
With gasoline wings
There's another road out of these rooms
Into the streets of elegant gawkers
Cafes have electric chairs now
And this is no road to travel
And this is the road to oblivion happiness
Cutup on the unknown and another acre of poems

Musick?
Here come the flagons of Isidore Ducasse
The speed which is happening
                                And the grave compassion

●

The riot was mainly in my mind
Soon I won't be here stretched out on pillows of imaginary iron
And the evil jinn leering into my dreams
I'm vanishing like vanishing letters
I can't bridge you reader you'll have to find yourself
Going on slow as the blood I see drop over us

●

Deflowering of technology
Beauty the suicide
Ice fevers
Wrapped around your head
Hers on fire

●

Even if supersonic sounds feed me with ithyphallic diseases and
    the roars of Aboreas
Was plain chant less tedious?
Answer me
Don't just stand there like the Tetragrammaton
This is truth
I'm obsessed by death fantasies
Husks
And the *Night Thoughts* of Edward Young

Death is a pineapple in the cake of death
Which wing?
I deny death I don't know why
Ask the swans who are rocking me under the chair forest

The dragon I saw
Small as my Jupiter finger
Looking back with miniature flames
The whole middle ages
And vanish quickly
Beauteous apparition I was thinking of war A poem
Beauty must be reckoned with

Penetrant Tumors

This is the U.S. penetrant tumors chopped with metal livers
The load of fairy fingers gesticulating war and the clothes wear-
    ing the people
Riding around the moon
They dream they dream
Their throats parched with dollar madness
This is the U.S. machine state
And a picnic in the fog is worth two in the vulva

Take a blood bath for breakfast
Drop the sirloin tip from the clouds
I've found the nut & bolt scratching the tide of suburban
    effluvia
Anesthetically wet
Let this never rest wild cock
This is America the enormous cemetery never to be discovered
But the slabs are singing cybernetic energy hydraulic energy

Don't eat the nylons off the women
Be firm and take over the corporations with dog pudding
India is looking away and Latin America is sleeping again
The Roman Empire keeps crunching into us in spite of the void
In spite of the alcoholic negotiations
In spite of melting candles on the Potomac
I'm patriotic as banzai
I identify continually with the hair style of George Washington
The filthy lucre games are almost ending
The invisibles are starving their unborn children at satellite sta-
    tions at Rome
Religion is just a big dumb con
Laugh your fill under the Papa's belly who has designs on Brazil
O well the idiots still dance to the technological arts
Heraclitus condemned most of them to the smoke chamber

What do pygmies chant on the silent hour telepathy TV?

Back to the essential cope
The U.S. is a work state on wheels
And I can't stop smoking imaginary French gardens put on with
    masonic ceremonies
I'm wondering about the Great Seal and the *novus ordo seclo-
rum*
The beautiful white mice in John Adams' elevator
Forever Our Fathers decree the classic sibyls
And the vengeance of Jacques de Molay
This is America a thousand islands of Gitchi Manito
Little progress since Iroquois cabals
The profits are yogic pins thru puritan cheeks
And the slobbering alcoholics
               flagging

(New Year 1969)

Letter to G: By some half-moon
       (6/18/68)   in Cancer 1968

The Analog

And the sea moved over the terrace into my marble stomach
that I saw the cleft on the rock disclose the Mason's Word
upon which were built the crumbling remains of Onn
treasure shored up from my inner eyes
the victuals medieval cathedrals secrete secretly
for the likes of the adepts
who smile through the velvet fissures of the centuries
that are Waves & Blankets of Stars
under which we are given, if we burrow long enough
for the hidden script, the Key to the King's Shut Chamber
that vanishes into the night hot with luminations
re-seered at the ice trance permitted to the high flyers
who with the correct gesture
at the right time know the precise moment
the Zodiac favors the conflagration of water and
the stillness of things about to become
when fire reabsorbs its opposite
the snarling snake before the plumage of the perfectly secured
      Peacock
Perchance the wave falls prematurely and spoils the little work
the Operator must beforehand arm himself with traditional
      shields
so that translated into the occult veins of his visible anatomy
the fox & falcon hoods spill volumes and sweat beacons
to throw him into the path which has no way up or down
and is never either way to the Ravaging Ferocious Mountain
  . . .Ah what am I saying that my lips might be burned by
      angels and sirens?

World without End

Now I will take hold of the wind as the tons of weeds tumble from the mouths of fountains, and I can not imagine any bodies but angels yes. Always the wind bears the breasts of the bottom stairway, my heart shall be in the roar of attention, attention to the open flood gate, only no other voice shall mewl. For the person shall be submerged & surpassed by the Head the talking Flower of Pure Vision. Let us enter the wind's mummy as if it were not less than Genius, as it is I affirm the trembling lyres of Lycophron are greater than Homer's. Let this pass through the pharaonic knot prepared in the communal future where the winds shall unlatch all the leaves.

I spurt the heavy odors of the sphincter's hair. Together the prairies of America are cornholed into the mouth of China which is greater & less crowded than Portugal for the scene of the eventual leap of frog-poets into the waters of the wind. They spill their craps & leagues of white mystics this second into your laps, my country pens & fowls from under the Echo I ring!

The dragon is real and more beautiful than the photos ever and invisible medieval cards which did not depict its flash of jeweled vision. The pearl of the dragon is the splendor of the night, night from the beginning the foremost declaration of the sun's freedom. To burn thee black, my pretty flame, all women are undressed before his loon laughter. He spits the bible that's read too fast to be seen and is the invisible tapestry of the coming race. Already the burning neons foam under the beds of the cowardly vampires whose holy grace spins the office of lies inverted from ashtrays of the mendicant orders. Don't be fooled again by the leech window from the swinging dead bodies lapped up by members of the mystical trust; their banks smolder under the backward resurrection which is sweet as ether. I continue to lure the wind's eye I am one with the wind. There are no other friends. The avalanche begins!

Fog from under torpor's side and its veins above my hand raid the chrysallis dawn drenches with the tears of the machine I wash by the orifice of the caldron where magicians lie cut by glass and ply the trade of trailing buddhas, where the orient maneuvers the moon's leg twisted on rails of honey. Bring the sarcophagus of the immortal wail. I unwrap the box of fears and nail the corridor of nude wonders below the street that smiles. Black fire slakes the fist of water below the winter loneliness into the spectral slum you made, my chicken lair of beauty's corpse.

Horn of the summer. Soon the immaculate harvest. Two precious stones too bright for any eye. Hear the silence I vanquish. Note the lugubrious hymen devoid of its rasp and bleeding the milk of the Sphinx.

I have come again to the gate where the pearl water kisses the mine of light inscaped with the flower of entrails I dreamed last night. The waterway vanishes when the pure font ceases in the crepuscular vine dinner of the day we abandon to enter the true temple that is some secret inner night never more revealed than by the flower of water breaking over brains, the hands I print with the pain erased with enigma & smile of the pure land shake.

Let it be said on the hysterical sublime of this moment: open all the doors to tomorrow's liberty. On the flight of my eyes from the depth chamber's heart attack stroke of the light forever below, the stomach I dreamt is to be purged of extraneous influences who came in my youth and undid my clear sight of the dragon rite.

Peace is knocked over with a slumber foot, the match hair, pumice of bleeding liver and core of orange light. Fingers of soul dash the flames from pure saliva's soap, my life at the sacrament of black underground river POETRY THE PUREST LIFE. The world is irrevocable, transmuted today, and never shall day claw me to sleep but night wake the salamander's pickaxe. I cleave open the paper wall. The blood-stained fingers are pushed to the vanishing full pardon of the river and I am salved with the unflickering beacon roaring from the magenta whorl floating through the veil of Hermes Trismegistus, the original voice come from under the wink of 40 centuries. You curl the lip of ziggurats, you warp the palaces of resurrection: the glorification murder is resplendent with the purifying death whose nose moves my hand through the chinks from the underworld. Hail, Prince of Panic, I tumble you under the war bit.

Newspapers disappear, current vices appear as smoke tissues salute the bodies of the enlightened before the past began to draw the curtain of dust on the total eclipse my contemporaries imagine. I am beginning to eat light, straight *and of the corner stone* sprung up, grail-of-the-betel-lady, swinger of the nymph conch veined with the pest, thunderwing who comes clothed with high noon. I vanish to start the sun to roll its eyes from the subterranean chant that is and knows no name, Mystery of the clock that prunes the transmutative glance Look out of weir window and glyph god from under the vomit's shield.

O delicate white fang O child of roe O caught in your beautiful knot of blood I set you free for the thunder's kiss and the white tree, madrone of your first year of the kill. Suck the bark to your star's ease that illumines One, the cavern above the storm Two, the desire which is desired, and Three phases from virginal to torture. This is my valentine too warm for the mails of the spirit and so I send it on a lunatic screen made of shimmering paste over invisible bridges.

The secret doe takes up the skin of forests and converts them to the willowy convulsions of Irawaka *and before* when all the machines were made of floating cream black ice and the husk of our fruitless tears. Certainly in the future I care nothing for it. I am writing this now for you, then. You keep creeping out of the rose lip, tobacco horrors and the lust for drugs. At the terminal cage I free you I repeat out of the sad sadism of left and right. No more self-inflicted ants, you're close to the coiled element, the supreme root of fire.

All the mancies shall be mine who grew the trunk from the vibrated seed sent from the sun, though it traveled around the hospitals of hatred before it touched the magnetic stone basin and toppled into place under your belly's surgical history O poor astral anatomy so long bludgeoned by occult blows. I'm on to the whole con, sweet sadists, you don't stop the eternal loin from speaking its ocean to be. I can barely see you mixed up to be chopped like so many valentine hearts by the fierce blades that I roll out of the black star!

Beat of the interior fleet, I unveil your head grown from the four children of Horus. The Lion driven out of Heliopolis, the masquerades of the apocalypse, the whispering vision and other conferences of the children of light shall be noted once here along with my return to Kohl Castle and the rock where I raped the sea. The mirrors recorded everything. They wear the flesh of the Lion's cage, he's freed from the object and his lair sacred, the only shrine I find, but thee, marvelous child wearing out your torturers under the shade of blinding water IT FALLS

rolls over on its ear. I would spit on the foam and drive it INTO THE CRASHES!

45